Published in the United States by BQB Publishing
(an imprint of Boutique of Quality Books Publishing Company)
www.bqbpublishing.com

Printed in the United States of America

978-1-945448300 (h)
978-1-945-448-31-7 (e)

Library of Congress Control Number: 2019938688

Cover and interior illustrations: Josh Hara
Interior Design Setup: Robin Krauss, www.bookformatters.com
Editor: Olivia Swenson

Frank:

I'd like to dedicate this book to anyone and everyone who has ever felt different or ashamed of themselves. Trust me when I say - you are far from being alone! Also to my son, Briggs - who is the light of my life and the inspiration for all of this.

Josh:

For Jonah and Izzy. Without you, I never would have been prepared for this moment. But the countless hours spent reading you picture books and stories gave me all the inspiration I needed. So, this is dedicated to you – and your mom, who has always taught you, above all else, the importance of being kind.

SOME PEOPLE
ARE DARK

SOME PEOPLE
ARE LIGHT

YOU MAY NOT KNOW THEM

THEY MAY NOT BE YOU,

BUT SOME PEOPLE ARE,

AND SOME PEOPLE DO.

SOME PEOPLE
ARE RICH

SOME
PEOPLE
ARE
POOR

SOME PEOPLE HAVE LESS

SOME PEOPLE HAVE MORE

SOME PEOPLE BUY STUFF,

MUCH MORE THAN THEY NEED.

SOME
PEOPLE
LIKE
CATS

SOME
PEOPLE
LIKE
DOGS

SOME
PEOPLE
LIKE
BOTH

SOME
PEOPLE
LIKE
HOGS!

BUT SOME PEOPLE ARE,

AND SOME PEOPLE DO.

SOME PEOPLE ARE THIN

SOME PEOPLE ARE PLUMP

Some People Don't Feel Quite Right in Their Skin

Some People Want Out of the Body They're In.

YOU MAY NOT KNOW THEM

THEY MAY NOT BE YOU,

BUT SOME PEOPLE ARE,

AND SOME PEOPLE DO.

SOME PEOPLE ARE SHORT

SOME PEOPLE ARE TALL

SOME PEOPLE FIT IN

SOME PEEPS NOT AT ALL

SOME PEOPLE FACE CHALLENGES OTHERS DON'T HAVE

SOME PEOPLE ARE SICK, OR UPSET, OR JUST SAD.

YOU MAY NOT KNOW THEM

THEY MAY NOT BE YOU,

BUT SOME PEOPLE ARE,

AND SOME PEOPLE DO.

SOME PEOPLE HAVE BOTH

OR JUST ONE

OR NOT ANY

33

SOME PEOPLE DON'T LIKE THE SAME THINGS THAT YOU DO.

BUT NONE OF THAT MATTERS—
AND THAT MUCH YOU KNOW.

SOME PEEPS UNDERSTAND NEW THINGS RIGHT AWAY

FOR OTHERS, IT COULD TAKE SEVERAL DAYS.

BUT SOME PEOPLE ARE,

AND SOME PEOPLE DO.

SOME PEOPLE WILL PRAY

TO SOMETHING ABOVE

SOME PEOPLE WILL NOT, BUT STILL EXPRESS LOVE

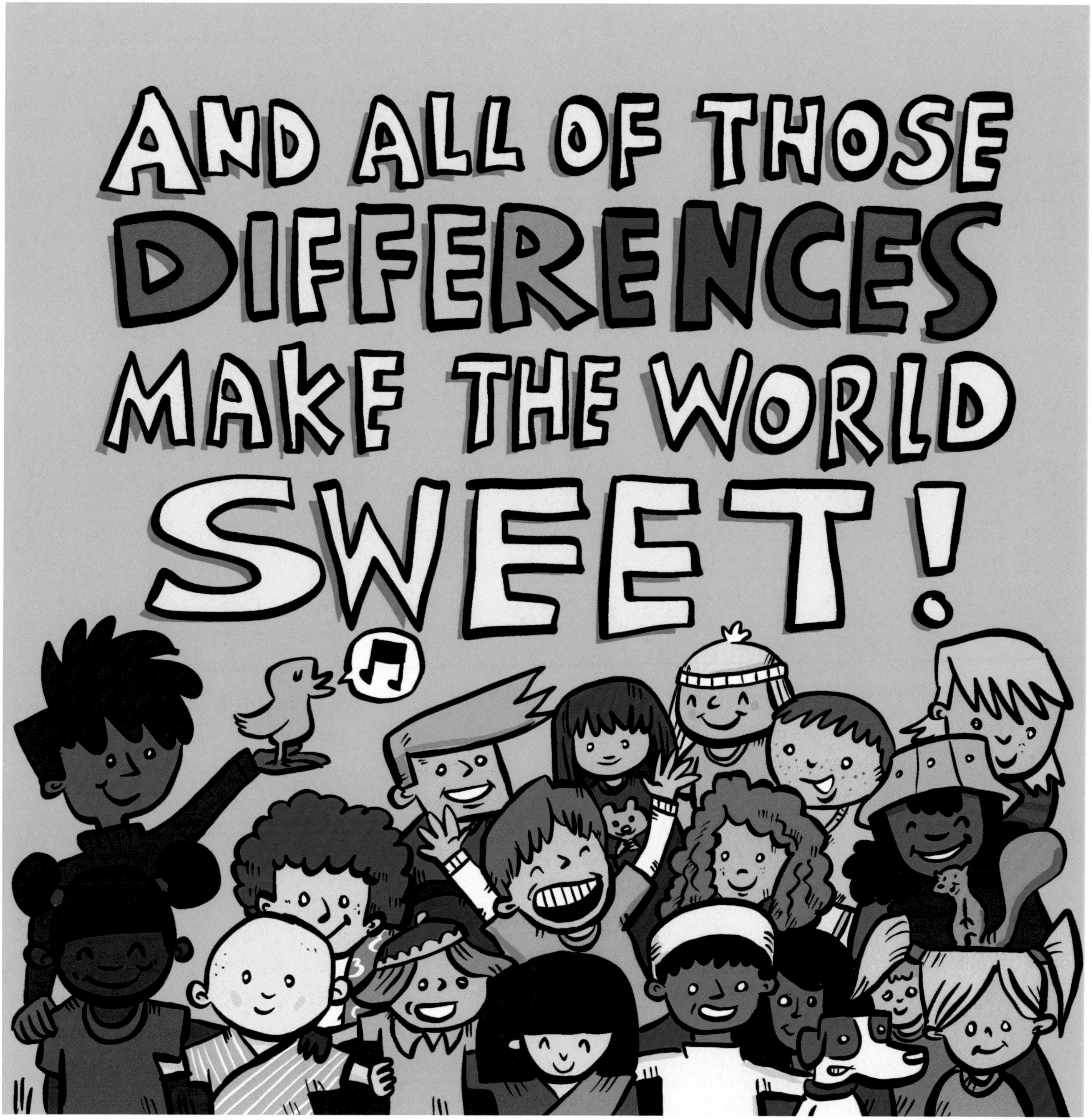
AND ALL OF THOSE
DIFFERENCES
MAKE THE WORLD
SWEET!

About the Author and Illustrator

Frank Lowe is a 42-year-old, gay, divorced dad. He is best known for his online personality @gayathomedad. He has written for major publications and released his first book (Editor, *Raised by Unicorns*) in 2018. His goal is to provide parents with easy tools to explain diversity to their children. *Some People Do* is his first children's book.

Josh Hara is a 46-year-old writer and illustrator that has a penchant for writing funny tweets and drawing on the sides of his coffee cups. Known across the internet as @yoyoha, Josh was thrilled when Frank contacted him about illustrating *Some People Do*. While studying art at the Columbus College of Art & Design (CCAD) Josh's first experience drawing children was in his retail illustration class. It was there he was taught the importance of inclusion, learning to respectfully represent children of all races, cultures and backgrounds. In *Some People Do* those early lessons have come to life more beautifully than ever before.